I0456644

The Spirit of Japan

The Spirit of Japan
Rabindranath Tagore

MINT EDITIONS

The Spirit of Japan was first published in 1916.

This edition published by Mint Editions 2021.

ISBN 9781513215846 | E-ISBN 9781513213842

Published by Mint Editions®

MINT
EDITIONS

minteditionbooks.com

Publishing Director: Jennifer Newens
Design & Production: Rachel Lopez Metzger
Project Manager: Micaela Clark
Typesetting: Westchester Publishing Services

I am glad to have this opportunity once more of speaking to you before I leave Japan. My stay here has been so short that one may think I have not earned my right to speak to you about anything concerning your country. I feel sure that I shall be told, that I am idealising certain aspects, while leaving others unnoticed, and that there are chances of my disillusionment, if I remain here for long. For I have known foreigners, whose long experience has made them doubtful about your moral qualifications,—even of your full efficiency in modern equipments of progress.

But I am not going to be brow-beaten by the authority of long experience, which is likely to be an experience of blindness carried through long years. I have known such instances in my own country. The mental sense, by the help of which we feel the spirit of a people, is like the sense of sight, or of touch,—it is a natural gift. It finds its objects, not by analysis, but by direct apprehension. Those who have not this vision, merely see events and facts, and not their inner association. Those who have no ear for music, hear sounds, but not the song. Therefore when, by the mere reason of the lengthiness of their suffering, they threaten to establish the fact of the tune to be a noise, one need not be anxious about music. Very often it is mistakes that require longer time to develop their tangles, while the right answer comes promptly.

You ask me how I can prove, that I am right in my confidence that I can see. My answer is, because I see something which is positive. There are others, who affirm that they see something contrary. It only shows, that I am looking on the picture side of the canvas, and they on the blank side. Therefore my short view is of more value than their prolonged stare.

It is a truism to say that shadows accompany light. What you feel, as the truth of a people, has its numberless contradictions,—just as the roundness of the earth is contradicted at every step by its hills and hollows. Those who can boast of a greater familiarity with your country than myself, can bring before me loads of contradictions, but I remain firm upon my vision of a truth, which does not depend upon its dimension, but upon its vitality.

At first, I had my doubts. I thought that I might not be able to see Japan, as she is herself, but should have to be content to see the Japan that takes an acrobatic pride in violently appearing as something else. On my first arrival in this country, when I looked out from the balcony of a house on the hillside, the town of Kobe,—that huge mass of corrugated iron roofs,—appeared to me like a dragon, with glistening scales, basking in the sun, after having devoured a large slice of the living flesh of the earth. This dragon did not belong to the mythology of the past, but of the present; and with its iron mask it tried to look real to the children of the age,—real as the majestic rocks on the shore, as the epic rhythm of the sea-waves. Anyhow it hid Japan from my view, and I felt myself like the traveller, whose time is short, waiting for the cloud to be lifted to have a sight of the eternal snow on the Himalayan summit. I asked myself,—"Will the dense mist of the iron age give way for a moment, and let me see what is true and abiding in this land?" I was enveloped in a whirlwind of reception, but I had my misgivings and thought that this might be a violent outbreak of curiosity,—or that these people felt themselves bound to show their appreciation of a man who had won renown from Europe, thus doing honour to the West in a vicarious form.

But the clouds showed rifts, and glimpses I had of Japan where she is true and more human. While travelling in a railway train I met, at a wayside station, some Buddhist priests and devotees. They brought their basket of fruits to me and held their lighted incense before my face, wishing to pay homage to a man who had come from the land of Buddha. The dignified serenity of their bearing, the simplicity of their devoutness, seemed to fill the atmosphere of the busy railway station with a golden light of peace. Their language of silence drowned the noisy effusion of the newspapers. I felt that I saw something which was at the root of Japan's greatness. And, since then, I have had other opportunities of reaching the heart of the people; and I have come to the conclusion, that the welcome which flowed towards me, with such outburst of sincerity, was owing to the fact that Japan felt the nearness of India to herself, and realised that her own heart has room to expand beyond her boundaries and the boundaries of the modern time.

I have travelled in many countries and have met with men of all classes, but never in my travels did I feel the presence of the human so distinctly as in this land. In other great countries, signs of man's power loomed large, and I saw vast organisations which showed efficiency in all their features. There, display and extravagance, in dress, in furniture, in costly entertainments, are startling. They seem to push you back into a corner, like a poor intruder at a feast; they are apt to make you envious, or take your breath away with amazement. There, you do not feel man as supreme; you are hurled against the stupendousness of things that alienates. But, in Japan, it is not the display of power, or wealth, that is the predominating element. You see everywhere emblems of love and admiration, and not mostly of ambition and greed. You see a people, whose heart has come out and scattered itself in profusion in its commonest utensils of everyday life in its social institutions, in its manners, that are carefully perfect, and in its dealings with things that are not only deft, but graceful in every movement.

What has impressed me most in this country is the conviction that you have realised nature's secrets, not by methods of analytical knowledge, but by sympathy. You have known her language of lines and music of colours, the symmetry in her irregularities, and the cadence in her freedom of movements; you have seen how she leads her immense crowds of things yet avoids all frictions; how the very conflicts in her creations break out in dance and music; how her exuberance has the aspect of the fullness of self-abandonment, and not a mere dissipation of display. You have discovered that nature reserves her power in forms of beauty; and it is this beauty which, like a mother, nourishes all the giant forces at her breast, keeping them in active vigour, yet in repose. You have known that energies of nature save themselves from wearing out by the rhythm of a perfect grace, and that she with the tenderness of her curved lines takes away fatigue from the world's muscles. I have felt that you have been able to assimilate these secrets into your life, and the truth which lies in the beauty of all things has passed into your souls. A mere knowledge of things can be had in a short enough time, but their spirit can only be acquired by centuries of training and self-control. Dominating nature from outside is a much simpler thing than making her your own in love's delight, which is a work of true genius. Your race has shown that genius, not by acquirements, but by creations; not by display of things, but by manifestation of its own inner being. This creative power there is in all nations, and it is ever active in getting hold of men's natures and giving them a form according to its ideals. But here, in Japan, it seems to have achieved its success, and deeply sunk into the minds of all men, and permeated their muscles and nerves. Your instincts have become true, your senses keen, and your hands have acquired natural skill. The genius of Europe has given her people the power of organisation, which has specially made itself manifest in politics and commerce and in coordinating scientific knowledge. The genius of Japan has given you the vision of beauty in nature and the power of realising it in your life. And, because of this fact, the power of organisation has come so easily to your help when you needed it. For the rhythm of beauty is the inner spirit, whose outer body is organisation.

All particular civilisation is the interpretation of particular human experience. Europe seems to have felt emphatically the conflict of things in the universe, which can only be brought under control by conquest. Therefore she is ever ready for fight, and the best portion of her attention is occupied in organising forces. But Japan has felt, in her world, the touch of some presence, which has evoked in her soul a feeling of reverent adoration. She does not boast of her mastery of nature, but to her she brings, with infinite care and joy, her offerings of love. Her relationship with the world is the deeper relationship of heart. This spiritual bond of love she has established with the hills of her country, with the sea and the streams, with the forests in all their flowery moods and varied physiognomy of branches; she has taken into her heart all the rustling whispers and sighing of the woodlands and sobbing of the waves; the sun and the moon she has studied in all the modulations of their lights and shades, and she is glad to close her shops to greet the seasons in her orchards and gardens and cornfields. This opening of the heart to the soul of the world is not confined to a section of your privileged classes, it is not the forced product of exotic culture, but it belongs to all your men and women of all conditions. This experience of your soul, in meeting a personality in the heart of the world, has been embodied in your civilisation. It is civilisation of human relationship. Your duty towards your state has naturally assumed the character of filial duty, your nation becoming one family with your Emperor as its head. Your national unity has not been evolved from the comradeship of arms for defensive and offensive purposes, or from partnership in raiding adventures, dividing among each member the danger and spoils of robbery. It is not an outcome of the necessity of organisation for some ulterior purpose, but it is an extension of the family and the obligations of the heart in a wide field of space and time. The ideal of "maitri" is at the bottom of your culture,—"maitri" with men and "maitri" with Nature. And the true expression of this love is in the language of beauty, which is so abundantly universal in this land. This is the reason why a stranger, like myself, instead of feeling envy or humiliation before these manifestations of beauty, these creations of love, feels a readiness to participate in the joy and glory of such revealment of the human heart.

And this has made me all the more apprehensive of the change, which threatens Japanese civilisation, as something like a menace to one's own person. For the huge heterogeneity of the modern age, whose only common bond is usefulness, is nowhere so pitifully exposed against the dignity and hidden power of reticent beauty, as in Japan.

But the danger lies in this, that organised ugliness storms the mind and carries the day by its mass, by its aggressive persistence, by its power of mockery directed against the deeper sentiments of heart. Its harsh obtrusiveness makes it forcibly visible to us, overcoming our senses,— and we bring to its altar sacrifices, as does a savage to the fetish which appears powerful because of its hideousness. Therefore its rivalry to things that are modest and profound and have the subtle delicacy of life is to be dreaded.

I am quite sure that there are men in your nation, who are not in sympathy with your national ideals; whose object is to gain, and not to grow. They are loud in their boast, that they have modernised Japan. While I agree with them so far as to say, that the spirit of the race should harmonise with the spirit of the time, I must warn them that modernising is a mere affectation of modernism, just as affectation of poesy is poetising. It is nothing but mimicry, only affectation is louder than the original, and it is too literal. One must bear in mind, that those who have the true modern spirit need not modernise, just as those who are truly brave are not braggarts. Modernism is not in the dress of the Europeans; or in the hideous structures, where their children are interned when they take their lessons; or in the square houses with flat straight wall-surfaces, pierced with parallel lines of windows, where these people are caged in their lifetime; certainly modernism is not in their ladies' bonnets, carrying on them loads of incongruities. These are not modern, but merely European. True modernism is freedom of mind, not slavery of taste. It is independence of thought and action, not tutelage under European schoolmasters. It is science, but not its wrong application in life,—a mere imitation of our science teachers who reduce it into a superstition absurdly invoking its aid for all impossible purposes.

Science, when it oversteps its limits and occupies the whole region of life, has its fascination. It looks so powerful because of its superficiality,— as does a hippopotamus which is very little else but physical. Science speaks of the struggle for existence, but forgets that man's existence is not merely of the surface. Man truly exists in the ideal of perfection, whose depth and height are not yet measured. Life based upon science is attractive to some men, because it has all the characteristics of sport;

it feigns seriousness, but is not profound. When you go a-hunting, the less pity you have the better; for your one object is to chase the game and kill it, to feel that you are the greater animal, that your method of destruction is thorough and scientific. Because, therefore, a sportsman is only a superficial man,—his fullness of humanity not being there to hamper him,—he is successful in killing innocent life and is happy. And the life of science is that superficial life. It pursues success with skill and thoroughness, and takes no account of the higher nature of man. But even science cannot tow humanity against truth and be successful; and those whose minds are crude enough to plan their lives upon the supposition, that man is merely a hunter and his paradise the paradise of sportsman, will be rudely awakened in the midst of their trophies of skeletons and skulls. For man's struggle for existence is to exist in the fullness of his nature,—not by curtailing all that is best in him and dwarfing his existence itself, but by accepting all the responsibilities of his spiritual life, even through death and defeat.

I do not for a moment suggest, that Japan should be unmindful of acquiring modern weapons of self-protection. But this should never be allowed to go beyond her instinct of self-preservation. She must know that the real power is not in the weapons themselves, but in the man who wields those weapons; and when he, in his eagerness for power, multiplies his weapons at the cost of his own soul, then it is he who is in even greater danger than his enemies.

Things that are living are so easily hurt; therefore they require protection. In nature, life protects itself within in coverings, which are built with life's own material. Therefore they are in harmony with life's growth, or else when the time comes they easily give way and are forgotten. The living man has his true protection in his spiritual ideals, which have their vital connection with his life and grow with his growth. But, unfortunately, all his armour is not living,—some of it is made of steel, inert and mechanical. Therefore, while making use of it, man has to be careful to protect himself from its tyranny. If he is weak enough to grow smaller to fit himself to his covering, then it becomes a process of gradual suicide by shrinkage of the soul. And Japan must have a firm faith in the moral law of existence to be able to assert to herself, that the Western nations are following that path of suicide, where they are smothering their humanity under the immense weight of organisations in order to keep themselves in power and hold others in subjection.

Therefore I cannot think that the imitation of the outward aspects of the West, which is becoming more and more evident in modern Japan, is essential to her strength or stability. It is burdening her true nature and causing weakness, which will be felt more deeply as time goes on. The habits, which are being formed by the modern Japanese from their boyhood,—the habits of the Western life, the habits of the alien culture,—will prove, one day, a serious obstacle to the understanding of their own true nature. And then, if the children of Japan forget their past, if they stand as barriers, choking the stream that flows from the mountain peak of their ancient history, their future will be deprived of the water of life that has made her culture so fertile with richness of beauty and strength.

What is still more dangerous for Japan is, not this imitation of the outer features of the West, but the acceptance of the motive force of the Western civilisation as her own. Her social ideals are already showing signs of defeat at the hands of politics, and her modern tendency seems to incline towards political gambling in which the players stake their souls to win their game. I can see her motto, taken from science, "Survival of the Fittest," writ large at the entrance of her present-day history—the motto whose meaning is, "Help yourself, and never heed what it costs to others"; the motto of the blind man, who only believes in what he can touch, because he cannot see. But those who can see, know that men are so closely knit, that when you strike others the blow comes back to yourself. The moral law, which is the greatest discovery of man, is the discovery of this wonderful truth, that man becomes all the truer, the more he realises himself in others. This truth has not only a subjective value, but is manifested in every department of our life. And nations, who sedulously cultivate moral blindness as the cult of patriotism, will end their existence in a sudden and violent death. In past ages we had foreign invasions, there had been cruelty and bloodshed, intrigues of jealousy and avarice, but they never touched the soul of the people deeply; for the people, as a body, never participated in these games. They were merely the outcome of individual ambitions. The people themselves, being free from the responsibilities of the baser and more heinous side of those adventures, had all the advantage of the heroic and the human disciplines derived from them. This developed their unflinching loyalty, their single-minded devotion to the obligations of honour, their power of complete self-surrender and fearless acceptance of death and danger. Therefore the ideals, whose seats were in the hearts of the people, would not undergo any serious change owing to the policies adopted by the kings or generals. But now, where the spirit of the Western civilisation prevails, the whole people is being taught from boyhood, to foster hatreds and ambitions by all kinds of means,—by the manufacture of half-truths and untruths in history, by persistent misrepresentation of other races and the culture of unfavourable sentiments towards them, by setting up memorials of events, very often false, which for the sake of humanity should be speedily forgotten, thus continually brewing evil menace towards neighbours and nations other than their own. This is poisoning the very fountain-head of humanity. It is discrediting the ideals, which were born of the lives of men, who were our greatest and best. It is holding up gigantic selfishness as the one universal religion for all nations of the world. We can take anything else from the hands of science, but not this elixir of moral death. Never think for a moment, that the hurts you inflict upon other races will not infect you, and the enmities you sow around your homes will be a wall of protection to you for all time to come. To imbue the minds of a whole people with an abnormal vanity of its own superiority, to teach it to take pride in its moral callousness and ill-begotten wealth, to perpetuate humiliation of defeated nations by exhibiting trophies won from war, and using these in schools in order to breed in children's minds contempt for others, is imitating the West where she has a festering sore, whose swelling is a swelling of disease eating into its vitality.

Our food crops, which are necessary for our sustenance, are products of centuries of selection and care. But the vegetation, which we have not to transform into our lives, does not require the patient thoughts of generations. It is not easy to get rid of weeds; but it is easy, by process of neglect, to ruin your food crops and let them revert to their primitive state of wildness. Likewise the culture, which has so kindly adapted itself to your soil,—so intimate with life, so human,—not only needed tilling and weeding in past ages, but still needs anxious work and watching. What is merely modern,—as science and methods of organisation,—can be transplanted; but what is vitally human has fibres so delicate, and roots so numerous and far reaching, that it dies when moved from its soil. Therefore I am afraid of the rude pressure of the political ideals of the West upon your own. In political civilisation, the state is an abstraction and relationship of men utilitarian. Because it has no roots in sentiments, it is so dangerously easy to handle. Half a century has been enough for you to master this machine; and there are men among you, whose fondness for it exceeds their love for the living ideals which were born with the birth of your nation and nursed in your centuries. It is like a child, who, in the excitement of his play, imagines he likes his playthings better than his mother.

Where man is at his greatest, he is unconscious. Your civilisation, whose mainspring is the bond of human relationship, has been nourished in the depth of a healthy life beyond reach of prying self-analysis. But a mere political relationship is all conscious; it is an eruptive inflammation of aggressiveness. It has forcibly burst upon your notice. And the time has come, when you have to be roused into full consciousness of the truth by which you live, so that you may not be taken unawares. The past has been God's gift to you; about the present, you must make your own choice.

So the questions you have to put to yourselves are these,—"Have we read the world wrong, and based our relation to it upon an ignorance of human nature? Is the instinct of the West right, where she builds her national welfare behind the barricade of a universal distrust of humanity?"

You must have detected a strong accent of fear, whenever the West has discussed the possibility of the rise of an Eastern race. The reason of it is this, that the power, by whose help she thrives, is an evil power; so long as it is held on her own side she can be safe, while the rest of the world trembles. The vital ambition of the present civilisation of Europe is to have the exclusive possession of the devil. All her armaments and diplomacy are directed upon this one object. But these costly rituals for invocation of the evil spirit lead through a path of prosperity to the brink of cataclysm. The furies of terror, which the West has let loose upon God's world, come back to threaten herself and goad her into preparations of more and more frightfulness; this gives her no rest and makes her forget all else but the perils that she causes to others, and incurs herself. To the worship of this devil of politics she sacrifices other countries as victims. She feeds upon their dead flesh and grows fat upon it, so long as the carcasses remain fresh,—but they are sure to rot at last, and the dead will take their revenge, by spreading pollution far and wide and poisoning the vitality of the feeder. Japan had all her wealth of humanity, her harmony of heroism and beauty, her depth of self-control and richness of self-expression; yet the Western nations felt no respect for her, till she proved that the bloodhounds of Satan are not only bred in the kennels of Europe, but can also be domesticated in Japan and fed with man's miseries. They admit Japan's equality with themselves, only when they know that Japan also possesses the key to open the floodgate of hell-fire upon the fair earth, whenever she chooses, and can dance, in their own measure, the devil dance of pillage, murder, and ravishment of innocent women, while the world goes to ruin. We know that, in the early stage of man's moral immaturity, he only feels reverence for the god whose malevolence he dreads. But is this the ideal of man which we can look up to with pride? After centuries of civilisation nations fearing each other like the prowling wild beasts of the night time; shutting their doors of hospitality; combining only for purpose of aggression or defence; hiding in their holes their trade secrets, state secrets, secrets of their armaments; making peace offerings to the barking dogs of each other with the meat which does not belong to them; holding down fallen races struggling to stand upon their feet; counting their safety only upon the feebleness of the rest of humanity; with their right hands dispensing religion to weaker peoples, while robbing them with their left,—is there anything in this to make us envious? Are we to bend our knees to the spirit of this civilisation, which is sowing broadcast over all the world seeds of fear, greed, suspicion, unashamed lies of its diplomacy, and unctuous lies of its profession of peace and good-will and universal brotherhood of Man? Can we have no doubt in our minds, when we rush to the Western market to buy this foreign product in exchange for our own inheritance? I am aware how difficult it is to know one's self; and the man, who is intoxicated, furiously denies his drunkenness; yet the West herself is anxiously thinking of her problems and trying experiments. But she is like a glutton, who has not the heart to give up his intemperance in eating, and fondly clings to the hope that he can cure his nightmares of indigestion by medicine. Europe is not ready to give up her political inhumanity, with all the baser passions of man attendant upon it; she believes only in modification of systems, and not in change of heart.

We are willing to buy their machine-made systems, not with our hearts, but with our brains. We shall try them and build sheds for them, but not enshrine them in our homes, or temples. There are races, who worship the animals they kill; we can buy meat from them, when we are hungry, but not the worship which goes with the killing. We must not vitiate our children's minds with the superstition, that business is business, war is war, politics is politics. We must know that man's business has to be more than mere business, and so have to be his war and politics. You had your own industry in Japan; how scrupulously honest and true it was, you can see by its products,—by their grace and strength, their conscientiousness in details, where they can hardly be observed. But the tidal wave of falsehood has swept over your land from that part of the world, where business is business, and honesty is followed in it merely as the best policy. Have you never felt shame, when you see the trade advertisements, not only plastering the whole town with lies and exaggerations, but invading the green fields, where the peasants do their honest labour, and the hill-tops, which greet the first pure light of the morning? It is so easy to dull our sense of honour and delicacy of mind with constant abrasion, while falsehoods stalk abroad with proud steps in the name of trade, politics and patriotism, that any protest against their perpetual intrusion into our lives is considered to be sentimentalism, unworthy of true manliness.

And it has come to pass, that the children of those heroes, who would keep their word at the point of death, who would disdain to cheat men for vulgar profit, who even in their fight would much rather court defeat than be dishonourable, have become energetic in dealing with falsehoods and do not feel humiliated by gaining advantage from them. And this has been effected by the charm of the word "modern." But if undiluted utility be modern, beauty is of all ages; if mean selfishness be modern, the human ideals are no new inventions. And we must know for certain, that however modern may be the proficiency, which clips and cripples man for the sake of methods and machines, it will never live to be old.

When Japan is in imminent peril of neglecting to realise where she is great, it is the duty of a foreigner like myself to remind her, that she has given rise to a civilisation which is perfect in its form, and has evolved a sense of sight which clearly sees truth in beauty and beauty in truth. She has achieved something, which is positive and complete. It is easier for a stranger to know what it is in her, which is truly valuable for all mankind,—what is there, which only she, of all other races, has produced from her inner life and not from her mere power of adaptability. Japan must be reminded, that it is her sense of the rhythm of life and of all things, her genius for simplicity, her love for cleanliness, her definiteness of thought and action, her cheerful fortitude, her immense reserve of force in self-control, her sensitiveness to her code of honour and defiance of death, which have given her the power to resist the cyclonic storm of exploitation that has sprung from the shores of Europe circling round and round the world. All these qualities are the outcome of a civilisation, whose foundation is in the spiritual ideals of life. Such a civilisation has the gift of immortality; for it does not offend against the laws of creation and is not assailed by all the forces of nature. I feel it is an impiety to be indifferent to its protection from the incursion of vulgarity of power.

But while trying to free our minds from the arrogant claims of Europe and to help ourselves out of the quicksands of our infatuation, we may go to the other extreme and blind ourselves with a wholesale suspicion of the West. The reaction of disillusionment is just as unreal as the first shock of illusion. We must try to come to that normal state of mind, by which we can clearly discern our own danger and avoid it, without being unjust towards the source of that danger. There is always the natural temptation in us of wishing to pay back Europe in her own coin, and return contempt for contempt and evil for evil. But that again would be to imitate Europe in one of her worst features which comes out in her behaviour to people whom she describes as yellow or red, brown or black. And this is a point on which we in the East have to acknowledge our guilt and own that our sin has been as great, if not greater, when we insulted humanity by treating with utter disdain and cruelty men who belonged to a particular creed, colour or caste. It is really because we are afraid of our own weakness, which allows itself to be overcome by the sight of power, that we try to substitute for it another weakness which makes itself blind to the glories of the West. When we truly know the Europe which is great and good, we can effectively save ourselves from the Europe which is mean and grasping. It is easy to be unfair in one's judgment when one is faced with human miseries,—and pessimism is the result of building theories while the mind is suffering. To despair of humanity is only possible, if we lose faith in the power which brings to it strength, when its defeat is greatest, and calls out new life from the depth of its destruction. We must admit that there is a living soul in the West which is struggling unobserved against the hugeness of the organisations under which men, women and children are being crushed, and whose mechanical necessities are ignoring laws that are spiritual and human,—the soul whose sensibilities refuse to be dulled completely by dangerous habits of heedlessness in dealings with races for whom it lacks natural sympathy. The West could never have risen to the eminence she has reached, if her strength were merely the strength of the brute, or of the machine. The divine in her heart is suffering from the injuries inflicted by her hands upon the world,—and from this pain of her higher nature flows the secret balm which will bring healing to those injuries. Time after time she has fought against herself and has undone the chains, which with her own hands she had fastened round helpless limbs; and though she forced poison down the throat of a great nation at the point of sword for gain of money, she herself woke up to withdraw from it, to wash her hands clean again. This shows hidden springs of humanity in spots which look dead and barren. It proves that the deeper truth in her nature, which can survive such career of cruel cowardliness, is not greed, but reverence for unselfish ideals. It would be altogether unjust, both to us and to Europe, to say that she has fascinated the modern Eastern mind by the mere exhibition of her power. Through the smoke of cannons and dust of markets the light of her moral nature has shone bright, and she has brought to us the ideal of ethical freedom, whose foundation lies deeper than social conventions and whose province of activity is world-wide.

The East has instinctively felt, even through her aversion, that she has a great deal to learn from Europe, not merely about the materials of power, but about its inner source, which is of mind and of the moral nature of man. Europe has been teaching us the higher obligations of public good above those of the family and the clan, and the sacredness of law, which makes society independent of individual caprice, secures for it continuity of progress, and guarantees justice to all men of all positions in life. Above all things Europe has held high before our minds the banner of liberty, through centuries of martyrdom and achievement,—liberty of conscience, liberty of thought and action, liberty in the ideals of art and literature. And because Europe has won our deep respect, she has become so dangerous for us where she is turbulently weak and false,—dangerous like poison when it is served along with our best food. There is one safety for us upon which we hope we may count, and that is, that we can claim Europe herself, as our ally, in our resistance to her temptations and to her violent encroachments; for she has ever carried her own standard of perfection, by which we can measure her falls and gauge her degrees of failure, by which we can call her before her own tribunal and put her to shame,—the shame which is the sign of the true pride of nobleness.

But our fear is, that the poison may be more powerful than the food, and what is strength in her today may not be the sign of health, but the contrary; for it may be temporarily caused by the upsetting of the balance of life. Our fear is that evil has a fateful fascination, when it assumes dimensions which are colossal,—and though at last, it is sure to lose its centre of gravity, by its abnormal disproportion, the mischief which it creates before its fall may be beyond reparation.

Therefore I ask you to have the strength of faith and clarity of mind to know for certain, that the lumbering structure of modern progress, riveted by the iron bolts of efficiency, which runs upon the wheels of ambition, cannot hold together for long. Collisions are certain to occur; for it has to travel upon organised lines, it is too heavy to choose its own course freely; and once it is off the rails, its endless train of vehicles is dislocated. A day will come, when it will fall in a heap of ruin and cause serious obstruction to the traffic of the world. Do we not see signs of this even now? Does not the voice come to us, through the din of war, the shrieks of hatred, the wailings of despair, through the churning up of the unspeakable filth which has been accumulating for ages in the bottom of this civilisation,—the voice which cries to our soul, that the tower of national selfishness, which goes by the name of patriotism, which has raised its banner of treason against heaven, must totter and fall with a crash, weighed down by its own bulk, its flag kissing the dust, its light extinguished? My brothers, when the red light of conflagration sends up its crackle of laughter to the stars, keep your faith upon those stars and not upon the fire of destruction. For when this conflagration consumes itself and dies down, leaving its memorial in ashes, the eternal light will again shine in the East,—the East which has been the birth-place of the morning sun of man's history. And who knows if that day has not already dawned, and the sun not risen, in the Easternmost horizon of Asia? And I offer, as did my ancestor rishis, my salutation to that sunrise of the East, which is destined once again to illumine the whole world.

I know my voice is too feeble to raise itself above the uproar of this bustling time, and it is easy for any street urchin to fling against me the epithet of "unpractical." It will stick to my coat-tail, never to be washed away, effectively excluding me from the consideration of all respectable persons. I know what a risk one runs from the vigorously athletic crowds to be styled an idealist in these days, when thrones have lost their dignity and prophets have become an anachronism, when the sound that drowns all voices is the noise of the market-place. Yet when, one day, standing on the outskirts of Yokohama town, bristling with its display of modern miscellanies, I watched the sunset in your southern sea, and saw its peace and majesty among your pine-clad hills,—with the great Fujiyama growing faint against the golden horizon, like a god overcome with his own radiance,—the music of eternity welled up through the evening silence, and I felt that the sky and the earth and the lyrics of the dawn and the dayfall are with the poets and idealists, and not with the marketsmen robustly contemptuous of all sentiments,— that, after the forgetfulness of his own divinity, man will remember again that heaven is always in touch with his world, which can never be abandoned for good to the hounding wolves of the modern era, scenting human blood and howling to the skies.

A Note About the Author

Rabindranath Tagore (1861–1941) was an Indian poet, composer, philosopher, and painter from Bengal. Born to a prominent Brahmo Samaj family, Tagore was raised mostly by servants following his mother's untimely death. His father, a leading philosopher and reformer, hosted countless artists and intellectuals at the family mansion in Calcutta, introducing his children to poets, philosophers, and musicians from a young age. Tagore avoided conventional education, instead reading voraciously and studying astronomy, science, Sanskrit, and classical Indian poetry. As a teenager, he began publishing poems and short stories in Bengali and Maithili. Following his father's wish for him to become a barrister, Tagore read law for a brief period at University College London, where he soon turned to studying the works of Shakespeare and Thomas Browne. In 1883, Tagore returned to India to marry and manage his ancestral estates. During this time, Tagore published his *Manasi* (1890) poems and met the folk poet Gagan Harkara, with whom he would work to compose popular songs. In 1901, having written countless poems, plays, and short stories, Tagore founded an ashram, but his work as a spiritual leader was tragically disrupted by the deaths of his wife and two of their children, followed by his father's death in 1905. In 1913, Tagore was awarded the Nobel Prize in Literature, making him the first lyricist and non-European to be awarded the distinction. Over the next several decades, Tagore wrote his influential novel *The Home and the World* (1916), toured dozens of countries, and advocated on behalf of Dalits and other oppressed peoples.

A Note from the Publisher

Spanning many genres, from non-fiction essays to literature classics to children's books and lyric poetry, Mint Edition books showcase the master works of our time in a modern new package. The text is freshly typeset, is clean and easy to read, and features a new note about the author in each volume. Many books also include exclusive new introductory material. Every book boasts a striking new cover, which makes it as appropriate for collecting as it is for gift giving. Mint Edition books are only printed when a reader orders them, so natural resources are not wasted. We're proud that our books are never manufactured in excess and exist only in the exact quantity they need to be read and enjoyed.

bookfinity™

Discover more of your favorite classics with Bookfinity™.

- Track your reading with custom book lists.
- Get great book recommendations for your personalized Reader Type.
- Add reviews for your favorite books.
- AND MUCH MORE!

Visit **bookfinity.com** and take the fun Reader Type quiz to get started.

Enjoy our classic and modern companion pairings!

Bookfinity is a registered trademark of Ingram Book Group LLC. © 2023 Bookfinity. All rights reserved.

www.ingramcontent.com/pod-product-compliance
Lightning Source LLC
Chambersburg PA
CBHW020324150626
46552CB00022B/3209